Be Phenomenal!

02/07/18

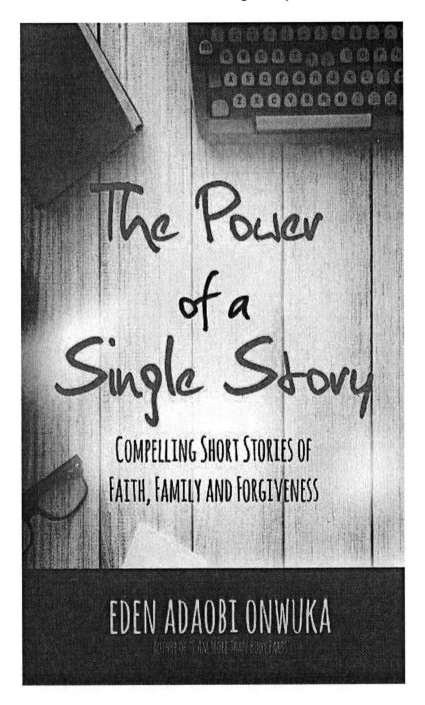

The Power
of a
Single Story

COMPELLING SHORT STORIES OF
FAITH, FAMILY AND FORGIVENESS

EDEN ADAOBI ONWUKA
AUTHOR OF "A LOT MORE THAN BODY PARTS"

Eden Adaobi Onwuka

The Power of a Single Story:
Compelling Short Stories of Faith, Family and Forgiveness

Eden Adaobi Onwuka

Pearly Gates
Publishing LLC
"Inspiring Christian Authors to BE Authors"

Pearly Gates Publishing, LLC, Houston, Texas

The Power of a Single Story:
Compelling Short Stories of Faith,
Family and Forgiveness

Scripture references marked KJV, NASB, and NIV are used
with permission from Zondervan via Biblegateway.com.

ISBN 13: 978-1-945117-98-5
Library of Congress Control Number: 2017960638

For information and bulk ordering, contact:
Pearly Gates Publishing, LLC
Angela R. Edwards, CEO
P.O. Box 62287
Houston, TX 77205
BestSeller@PearlyGatesPublishing.com

DEDICATION

To the Spirit of God,
without Whom I'd remain an Unwritten Sage.

For my Father and First Cheerleader:
Sir Ike Chris Stanley Udemgba {KSM}.

The Power of a Single Story

PREFACE

I believe with all my heart that we all experience remarkable events on a daily basis. Living in a fast-paced world, we either gloss over them or never even notice them; yet even as we pay close attention to them, they can become defining moments and strong references. Like Albert Einstein said, *"There are two ways to live: You can live as if nothing is a miracle or you can live as if everything is a miracle"*.

These Faith-based short stories are true stories, intentionally captured to reflect the miracles that can happen to us daily. These stories were inspired by an unplanned iPad selfie, which later became 'The Story Behind the Picture'. It is an exciting way of tackling some important issues about our time — a few of which were shared on a private women's forum and sparked a Faith revolution, brought about healing, and even spurred self-acceptance. So, I decided to share them in a book so that more people could enjoy and be enriched by them.

The Power of a Single Story is a fusion between fiction and non-fiction; the first volume of what I will call 'semi-fiction', which I would describe as the art of creatively telling a true story in such a way that it still has the literary elements of a non-fictional prose. This is no ordinary book, but transformational messages delivered with excellence and creativity.

If your Faith needs a picker-upper, this book is for you.

If you have ever experienced the despair that comes with infertility and delays, this book is for you.

If you've found yourself in a cycle of failed relationships, this book is for you.

If you have felt the stings of betrayal and rejection, this book is for you.

If you need a little push to make that next destiny move, this is it.

If you love a great read, a good laugh, and fun tales about family, this book is for you.

If in spite of everything you've been through, you hold on to some belief in Serendipity, then this book is for you.

The Power of a Single Story: Incomplete, but not inconsequential. Don't wait until you have it all to tell it all.

Stop holding back. There is POWER in YOUR story!

~ Eden A. Onwuka ~

Eden Adaobi Onwuka

TABLE OF CONTENTS

CHAPTER #1
The Story Behind the Picture

"For it is on troubled waters, that the strength of a sailing ship is weighed."

It was a cold, chilly December 31st in Nebraska. The snow had made a neat, foamy frost — the kind that would leave deep shoe imprints if one dared walk on it. It was one of those year ends when all you wanted to do was hunker down on the bed and snuggle under a warm blanket; one of those days when you felt neither excitement nor anti-climax, numb with the subtle dread for the incoming New Year. Enter in the familiar drill: adrenaline pumping, high expectations, lofty goals, and resolutions that fizzle out mid-year into a steady routine. By the end of the year, that routine crashes head-on into a reality check. There's a numbness you hold guardedly for fear that if you did not, you would bubble over with false hope or topple over with deep dope.

This was another New Year's Eve, and I was preparing for a vigil on some countryside in a land far from where I called 'home'. Long before selfies and selfie-sticks, I paused, let out a sigh, looked up, and took a picture. I stared at my reflection in the mirror and managed a weak, accomplished smile.

The significance of the moment was that it represented everything that wasn't, everything I wasn't, and everything I somehow hoped would be. I was in a transition; confused, alone, second-guessing my decision to move millions of miles away from home, and unsure of where my next rent payment would come from. I was barely surviving under a tight budget that felt "broker than broke".

Wearing a dress given to me by a dear friend that Christmas, I was able to make the impromptu trip; a pseudo vacation to the countryside by the sheer benevolence of my twin sister who had purchased my flight ticket. I was hosted by a woman I'd known for only a few hours who let me use her guest room for a few days—a kind woman named Franca, whom I met through my childhood friend.

There I was: facing my fears and taking a leap of faith to boldly move in the direction of my dreams. I had enrolled in a graduate program my perceived 'un-analytical mind' (at the time) wished I hadn't signed up for. Barely two months earlier, I was on some compulsory diet. It wasn't a fancy Mediterranean diet with exotic celebrities doubling as Brand Ambassadors. It wasn't a tested, trusted diet that promised the loss of abs while eating carbs. My diet was a situational one: noodles. They were what I could conveniently afford.

I remember the look [of pity?] on my roommates' faces when I would prep my noodles for breakfast, lunch, and dinner in the narrow kitchen we shared. Meanwhile, the vibrant and rich aroma of rich Indian cuisine sautéed in a bed of vegetables and spices greeted my nostrils. I still chuckle as I recall the half-amused look my roommate Priya had when I vehemently tried to convince her that my preference for noodles was a new nutritional fad. She didn't seem convinced.

So, unsure of what the next season of my life would bring, I kept asking myself, *"Girl, who put you up to this?"* or (in 'Pidgin English') *"Who send me message?"*

> *Broken or wrong relationships have a way of making you question your validity.*

Earlier that year, I had broken off an engagement — one in which I felt strongly that I was "settling" — and decided to step out of my comfort zone alone to pursue my dreams. Although it was my decision, it left me feeling lonely and afraid of yet again attracting the wrong 'type' of man. I silently wondered, *"Am I the wrong 'type' of woman?"*

You see, broken or wrong relationships have a way of making you question your validity. It doesn't matter if you walked out or if the "significant other" walked away; any walking may leave you initially feeling ousted.

> *"Then the LORD God took the man and put him into the Garden of Eden to cultivate it and keep it."*
>
> (Genesis 2:15, NASB)

I prayed that scripture for as long as I can remember, adapting the Garden of 'Eden' to be me, and the 'man' to be a man best-suited for me. For several years, I asked God to gift me with a 'Nurturer'—a man who, in partnership, will tend and cultivate my dreams. In between, I got all kinds of men.

So, on this particular New Year's Eve, I was tempted to end the year on a deep low, feed my fears, and starve my gratitude. It seemed the appropriate thing to do, right? Sure!

No income, funds, or rent money.

No family close by.

No relationship.

No plans outside of the immediate.

In debt for my graduate program.

Lonely.

Cold.

Hangry (hungry + angry = **HANGRY**)!

Oh. I can't forget: a tad bit scared.

In the end, I made a firm decision: Be Grateful. Grateful for life. Grateful for doing it afraid. Grateful for the uncomfortable present.

I hurriedly got ready to go with my host, Franca, to the vigil to serve my heart out. She and I had spent the better part of the day cooking for the guests who would attend the vigil, and I was excited to serve those who seemed to "have it all". Even though I didn't have much, surely, I could serve those who represented everything I had yet to attain.

Exactly one year from the date the photo was taken, I finished my MBA on the Dean's List in the Fourth Module AND met-dated-courted-married my 'Nurturer'; a man who exceeded my wildest dreams of both honor and integrity.

By a stroke of Divine intersection, I obtained a rent-free room, from a kind lady named Joy, for the remainder of the program.

That same year, I enjoyed two all-expense paid trips to Disneyland, was no longer alone, and had a new family of friends, teammates, and a kind church family.

I kid you not: The storm is not beautiful. The storm can be treacherous, boisterous, and intimidating. Although there may be no beauty in the storm, I have learned to choose to be beautiful in the storm.

I was right in the midst of my own storm, holding on to dreams without strategy and faith without a sign. That unpredictable season of transition was captured by an almost picture-perfect shot. You can credit the angle, lighting, camera, or makeup for the outcome of that random shot. I credit God — and having the right attitude. When you choose to serve others, to love, and to be thankful for the little you have (despite the fear around you), you, too, will be beautiful in the storm.

The fact that the unplanned bathroom selfie reflected a beauty that was non-existent in my reality simply meant **'Our Storms Don't Define Us — And It Shouldn't Confine Us'**. If we dare to look up when we could easily look back (with regret), look down (in defeat), or look around (in fear), we will eventually prevail over the storm! And the storm? It soon passes on because you are a *Storm Trooper*, *Storm Chaser*, and *Storm Tamer*! Every storm has a lifespan called "Temporary".

PEN THE POWER OF YOUR STORY

What has a recent storm or challenge taught you?

_____

_____

_____

_____

_____

_____

_____

_____

_____

_____

_____

_____

_____

_____

Write a story around a picture of yours.

_____

_____

_____

_____

_____

_____

_____

_____

_____

_____

_____

_____

_____

_____

_____

_____

When, where, and why was that picture taken?

_____

_____

_____

_____

_____

_____

_____

_____

_____

_____

_____

_____

_____

_____

_____

CHAPTER #2
The Difference a Year Can Make

"Faith is evidence and substance first planted within our hearts that we may transplant them into our lives."

I stood up right in the middle of Joyce Meyer's teaching in response to a question she had asked. The auditorium was crowded. Bright halogen lights shone brightly as they hung from huge lamps that were tethered to the high ceiling of the dome we were in. You might be asking, *"Why did she stand? Was she supposed to be standing?"* To be honest, I had no business standing at all.

Glancing around me, trying not to be self-conscious but barely able to stay composed, I knew in my heart it was my moment, my time, no excuses, neither the time to allow 'reputation' to override passion nor let fear limit my faith. I stood as 'tall' as my 5-foot-something inches would allow. I stood for what I believed in my heart and for all I was praying for.

Hubby and I were trying for a baby, trusting and believing God to bless our bedroom 'gymnastics' (if you are like me and weren't exactly a "Spring Chicken" when you got hitched by **not** marrying in your teens, 20s, or early 30s, you soon realize that it seems like you're in a biological race for time). There is a continuous, never-ending race our humanity imposes on us — along with those we impose on ourselves. And though meeting hubby was nothing short of a beautiful story of God's grace; much like every good thing that comes our way, I was learning that it takes Faith to walk through the very doors my faith opened in the first place.

> *You'll need Faith to walk through the doors your Faith opened in the first place.*

Continuing on…

So, we met, fell in love, got married, and while enjoying married life, started trying for a baby. Each month, my cycle let me know we'd have to wait for the next cycle…and the next. For anyone hoping for a baby, you can understand the letdown with each monthly period (or what felt more like a 'RED' card). Like a stern-faced referee in a soccer game, that 'RED' sign was held up automatically disqualifying me from playing in the game. There were crushed dreams, silent sighs, feigned brave shrugs, and almost dismissive responses to well-wishers who prodded, *"When are you going to call us to eat Jollof rice?"*

You might ask, *"How long had you been waiting?"* My answer would be, **"Long enough!"** I remind women not to belittle another woman's 'wait' or experience just because we feel their wait doesn't reverberate with us. Delay is a reality everyone experiences; some longer than others. Society has somewhat made us think that if the wait does not have some type of dramatic twist to it or if it does not have a "number" of years, then it's not worth the narrative. I kindly disagree. I have talked to people whose one-year wait was as intense and heartbreaking as those in a one-month or 10-year wait.

> *Delay is a reality everyone experiences; some longer than others.*

Waiting is waiting. The arduous burden of not knowing when it will end and the helpless realization that you have little or no control over the outcome is an emotion shared by all those who are waiting must endure. Therefore, we must honor and respect the travail of others.

But I digress.

So, on this day—February 10th—Joyce Meyer was teaching on **PROCESS** and used pregnancy as the analogy. While driving her point home about each stage of conception having different presentations and outcomes, she asked, *"If you're here and you're pregnant, could I ask that you please stand* *up?"* I stood up—and no, I wasn't pregnant. No, my standing wasn't a lie or an attempt at falsehood. I felt a tug in my heart and a stirring in my spirit. I looked over at hubby sitting beside me and said, *"My love, I want us to take this by* Faith!*"* He nodded a silent yet strong affirmation. He held my hands in agreement, and I stood…for **US**.

> *When you feel a tug in your heart and a stirring in your spirit, just yield.*

After the service that day, I bought a pink Bible from the bookstore and wrote a congratulatory message in it to myself. It read:

"February 10. Double Divine Conception!"

My hubby and I began to specifically trust God for twin babies. A year prior, my husband's cousin (who donates handmade teddy bears to orphanages) hosted us to lunch. I saw some of those teddies and took two out of the lot, jokingly saying to her that they represented our future babies. In line with our new prayer focus, I went back to the suitcase where I had stored the teddy bears and brought them out. I laid them nicely on the bed in the spare room and began speaking to my future 'Twin Babies', using the teddies as a token of Faith.

From then onwards, hubby and I would talk to each other like we already had children. He would call in from work and ask about 'the twins'. In response, I would let him speak to them over the phone. Sometimes, I would put 'them' in front of the television in the living room to watch Mickey Mouse Clubhouse. It seemed corny and silly at first, and even funny as we progressed; however, we soon grew comfortable with it because for us, our actions held a deeper significance. It was an expression of our Faith. We owned our Faith, declared our Faith, and thanked God in advance for it.

> *Faith is a personal declaration of your expectations based on Divine promise; not human premise.*

I can understand the buzz that might be running through your thoughts at this moment. Maybe you find yourself thinking, *"What was the guarantee? Doesn't that seem a bit odd? Didn't you feel a little foolish? Isn't it too far-fetched?"* Or perhaps you are grappling with the facets of a failed experience you might have witnessed, and your reaction is: 'Someone I know did something like this and nothing happened'. I get it.

Honestly, I do—and you would not be wrong. However, I am learning that Faith is very personal.

Your Faith is a personal declaration of your own beliefs and expectations from sovereignty based on Divine promise; not human premise. The reason some of us sabotage our Faith, dreams, and goals is because we *CARE* too much. We care about what people will think or say. We care about how we might appear to others. What if "it" doesn't happen? What if we have to eat our words? **Who cares?**

> *Preoccupation with being politically-correct will leave you second-guessing yourself and limiting your Faith.*

I had long ago decided that my own Faith does not have a reputation. My Faith has no etiquette. My Faith isn't conformist. My Faith is unapologetic. My Faith is not expressed for the applause of men; rather it is for a just cause!

Two months later, I kept having these nagging headaches that would not go away, coupled with a slight fever that seemed to peak in the evening hours. Fearing I had come down with a bacterial infection or allergies, I made a visit to our family doctor. He ran a couple of random tests. We were pleasantly surprised when the hospital called to tell us I was *NOT* sick; I was almost six weeks pregnant! We were very excited! The rest of the pregnancy seemed to go fast, taking its toll on my strength and looks. For the most part, I was strong — except for intense cravings, headaches, and waist pains.

When the six-month mark came, we had a slight scare. I started bleeding slightly. I was so afraid of losing the baby and became so confused. I prayed with everything I had in me and called my Obstetrics/Gynecologist. We were instructed to come into the hospital immediately. While waiting for hubby to pick me up, I had a moment all by myself in the bathroom. As I stared at my reflection (with it staring right back at me), I remembered these words:

> *"And <u>these signs shall follow</u> those that believe: In my name, they shall cast out demons..."*
>
> Mark 16:17a, KJV *(Emphasis added)*

I could not shake off the words 'and these signs shall follow'. It was a lightbulb moment for me. I had spent the last two hours constantly checking to see the blood, obsessed with the bleeding, anxious because of the bleeding, and allowing it to communicate to me that I was losing my baby. All along, it was just a sign. I screamed aloud, **"I DON'T FOLLOW THE SIGNS; SIGNS FOLLOW ME! I DON'T FOLLOW SIGNS! SIGNS ARE NOT MY COMPASS!** If I keep moving in the direction of Faith, then signs (which are a byproduct of believing) move towards ME!" Faith breeds peace; not desperation. So, I took a shower and continued making my declarations.

> *We sabotage our Faith, our dreams, and our goals when we care too much about public opinion.*

My hubby finally arrived, and we made the trip to the hospital. I was moved to the Emergency Room triage where my heartrate and fetus were monitored closely. An oxygen mask was placed over my face because I had shortness of breath. After a series of tests and despite the intense pain I felt in my pelvic area, the results came back good. The bleeding was not a result of any ruptured membrane. Although the baby was slightly frazzled in my womb, there was no risk. Pain medications were prescribed, and I was discharged within 24 hours.

In November of that same year, we were blessed with our first child. We were overjoyed! Our hearts knew a purity of love that only a child could bring. Born 22 hours, five minutes, and four seconds after her daddy's birthday, Heaven had given us a worthy birthday gift for him. Life couldn't have been more beautiful. When our daughter was in her second year, we started trying for another pregnancy. For some reason, we continued hoping and Faith-ing for our twins. Soon, we found out we were pregnant again!

In September of the following year, I went for my first prenatal ultrasound. I laid on the examining table with my thoughts racing and an overwhelming tiredness from being stuck in traffic enroute to my appointment. I almost fell as my obstetrician's voice cut through my thoughts. He teasingly asked, *"Is this your first ultrasound?"* (He knew it wasn't; he helped birth my daughter.) His teasing continued: *"So, you don't know you're pregnant with twins?"*

What did he just say? With **WHAT**? I blinked my eyes and parted my lips, preparing to speak. I couldn't find any words to say. I stared hard at the ultrasound monitor and saw two hazy features; little round heads. Shell-shocked, I looked at Dr. Gene and managed to choke out the following words: *"Umm... You can't joke with stuff like this!"* He smiled reassuringly and said, *"I know it's funny because you've always talked about having twins and constantly teased ME about checking* *for a second baby during your first pregnancy. So, I'm kind of amazed it's actually happening!"* At that moment, all kinds of emotions overwhelmed me. A thousand songs filled my soul. I could not explain what I was feeling as I looked from the doctor to the monitor to my hubby, whose face was flushed with pure excitement. With tears streaming down my face and a heart filled with gratitude, hubby squeezed my hands and I mouthed to him: *"Papa Ejima. Baba Ibeji."*

> *"For the foolishness of God is wiser than human wisdom, and the weakness of God is stronger than human strength."*
> 1 Corinthians 1:25, NIV

A few people have said, *"I guess it runs in your family, seeing you have an identical twin sister yourself"* ... and they wouldn't be wrong—in a sense. This is not an attempt to downplay the place of medical science or genetics. What I do say in response, however, is: This right here is Prophetic over Genetic! I know our twins did not come exclusively on the heels of science because, irrespective of genetics, hereditary factors, etc., getting pregnant is not guaranteed. I believe it was an act of mercy; a Great God reaching down to encourage the Faith of two ordinary people so that many others who hear our story can be encouraged to birth their own testimony.

Our Leap Year twin babies arrived on February 29th. To the glory of God, our journey of Faith (which started years prior when I stood up in a conference) finally culminated in a miracle.

In one of my moments of doubt when I kept wondering when my shift was going to happen, when in an instant, I focused on my age, the passing of time, and got sidetracked by numbers, God comforted me with these profound words:

"I AM Kairo-logical; not chronological.
I created time, I dwell in time, I can work with time.
But I am not bound by time because I AM TIME."

I encourage you: Don't place an expiration date on your FAITH and dreams. Don't give in and don't give up just yet. Perhaps you may be ending the year "unusually" because of the loss or absence of a loved-one or a prized dream. Or maybe you or someone you know is trying for their own baby(ies). They may well be into their 30s, 40s, or even 50s. Some might be hoping to get married, and age seems to go up and never come down. Whatever side of the divide your desires place you, I believe your steadfast Faith will produce. Best of all, when you meet the spouse best-suited for you, chronology, sociology, mythology, or geography will not be an issue because **Kairos** time—the set time of Divine favor—overrides all other time zones.

> *"And this is the victory that has overcome the world.*
> *YOUR FAITH."*
> 1 John 5:4b, NIV

Don't stop now. Go ahead and speak prophetically, dream audaciously, love immensely, and live unapologetically. Let no recession affect your confession. Remember this: Faith honors God...and God honors Faith! He is a Redeemer who knows how to redeem years of waiting and make up for lost time.

I live by this principle and mantra: *If God does it, let Him take all the glory; and if He doesn't do it, I won't take the shame.* Either way, there's no liability.

If God does it, let Him take all the glory; and if He doesn't do it, I won't take the shame.

PEN THE POWER OF YOUR STORY

In your own words, describe what Faith means to you.

_____

_____

_____

_____

_____

_____

_____

_____

_____

_____

_____

_____

_____

_____

Write a story about how you received something you believed for.

_____

_____

_____

_____

_____

_____

_____

_____

_____

_____

_____

_____

_____

_____

_____

Write about an experience when your faith in God did not produce the expected outcome.

_____

_____

_____

_____

_____

_____

_____

_____

_____

_____

_____

_____

_____

_____

_____

_____

CHAPTER #3
My Future Self

"What lies behind us and what lies before us are small matters compared to what lies within us."
~ Ralph Waldo Emerson ~

Once upon a time, I was a magnet for wrong relationships. I thought it would remain my lot to attract excuse-givers, non-committal men, and outright preys. They cycle was the same: They always showed up before their baggage showed up. *"Awon 'agberos."* From the ex who kept stringing me along while talking to me from his jail cell in London, to the one whose father was some sort of juju priest cum voodoo consultant (and he, the voodoo intern parading as a clergy man suitor). My love life was the stuff of home videos, Investigative ID's 'My Crazy Ex' series, and Baba Suwe-land.

I knew loneliness, betrayal, rejection, the whole nine yards. My emotions were a rollercoaster, crashing into everything in its path. After another heartbreak, a betrayal by a close relative (which degenerated into a local scandal), and an engagement I broke off for fear I was getting married to the man for all the wrong reasons (as mentioned in Chapter One), I took an inventory of my heart. I confronted myself with the truth: I knew in my heart that all along, I had been attaching myself to available choices just for the temporary fix it seemed to give my empty heart and for the futile pursuit of the imaginary plaque of "Mrs." that our society wrongly amplifies.

> *Vision is a projection of a picture-perfect future in an imperfect moment.*

I made a decision: I decided to take my power back and rediscover my purpose once again over and beyond the pursuit of meaningless relationships. I knew deep down, beneath all the layers of my mess and hidden outside the self-limiting beliefs, there had to be more for me out there. So, I took a good look at the woman I could become if I gave her the permission to blossom—the one waiting on the fringes for her clipped wings to sprout again. I wrote "that woman" a letter. And though I was yet to discover the import of my writing to the future version of myself, I knew that Habakkak 2 verse 2 said, *"Write the **vision** down and make it plain, so that all who **read** it will **run** with it"*.

Dear Woman,

I know where you are now, but I also know you have destiny calling for you.

Determine to live vibrantly as a single, wholesome person. Gift the world with the change agent that you are, not one who is merely existing and waiting for that slow-paused choreographed social media moment when a man gets down on bended knee with a ring in the presence of onlookers and friends – while you gasp and cry with reckless relief or feigned surprise. Live beyond glossy lips, well-manicured limbs, and twerking hips. Let your life count more than the expectation of exotic rendezvous and fine-dining.

Decide that hiding behind your roles as a cover-up for ineptitude will no longer do. Decide that a desire for motherhood alone is no longer 'just enough'. Decide that becoming a wife is not some prized trophy or oversized accomplishment. Understand that your sexuality is a beautiful, integral part of you; not the sum of you. Strive to become everything you were created to be, unleashing your gifts and emptying yourself of every dormant potential before you die. Refuse to dim your cause in a flurry of never-ending chores.

Decide that your generation will find a 'savior' in you. Determine that every negative bulk of those gone by stops with you. Take the bold steps your great-grandmama, grandmama, and mama were afraid to take (regardless of what they told you, they are secretly hoping that you do). Disengage yourself from anything that seeks to steal your voice and desecrate your vision. Liberate yourself from mental slavery and the allure of limited sight.

Determine that your life will count for something bigger than you. Work hard. Work smart. Read. Learn a trade. Pray. Love. Sing. Dance. Travel. Discover. Explore. Stand tall. Cry. Laugh loudly. Dream. Begin again. Start now. Hope one more time. Rest. Reach out. Speak out. Ask; don't beg. Get back up alive. Stop spinning familiar barriers like a tired shawl. Stop telling your hushed stories in insignificant circles. Rise to the realization that you have been entrusted the privilege of being a co-creator; a bringer of life, a nurturer of dreams, a multiplier of seed, a sustainer of hope, a carrier of posterity, and a birther of purpose. You are more than enough. You alone determine what "enough" is.

Decide that you will stand after you fall. Refuse to wallow in a party of self-pity. Fail if you must, but don't remain in a perpetual state of failure. Don't make a pedestal out of any crutch meant to temporarily support you. Decide not to allow a rough season of negative feedbacks to turn into a lifetime of unfortunate clap-backs. Setbacks are seasonal, and despair has a deadline. You can live beyond that shame and scandal. Give it some time; it will no longer be 'Breaking News'. You can find beauty after the hell you've been through. You must permit yourself to renew, revive, and live again.

Nothing can withstand a woman with an elevated perspective and a determined mind — especially a woman who refuses to allow her spirit to become calcified by the hate all around her. Become that woman who finds strength in the journey after the pain that ripped through the soles of her tired feet; yet, despite her pain, she chooses to love and help others ease their pain.

Nothing can continually break the will of a woman who understands her worth, accepts she is worthy, and knows the majesty of her God.

Woman, Rise! Unveil! Unearth! Become!

Signed

~ Eden

This letter I wrote to my future self was penned from a place of pain. I was stuck in a cycle of soul-ties, weighed down by the desire for vindication at a time when there was no need to look ahead. It would have been easier to settle for the predictable, hide behind the safety of bitterness and unforgiveness, give up on good breaks, and count out all good men. My younger sisters were already married with children, so I had become the 'Aunty Asoebi' by default, and I was genuinely happy for them. I served sacrificially at their weddings with all my heart.

> *I believe we can find a way to draw courage, even from a place of discouragement.*

However, within our cultural context, being the 'Ada' (first of four daughters) seemed to amplify the narrative that my time was most certainly almost up. My praying mother never gave up on her belief that there was beauty in my future. Even then, I knew I needed to play a role in my deliverance, so I painfully let my heart ache and temporarily weaned myself off 'relationships', which allowed me to focus tirelessly on investing in my personal growth.

I believe we can find a way to draw courage, even from a place of discouragement. I also believe we can love from a place of pain.

Several broken hearts later, some deep betrayals, and a broken engagement, I had the boldness to move intercontinentally as God stirred it in my heart to do. After a series of events which began at a random Thanksgiving party in Boston, Massachusetts, well into my 30s, I met my dream man. Relocating was not an easy decision because it meant I had to leave the comfort of the familiar: a good job, family, friends, and structure. I couldn't help but recall how many well-meaning people had thought I was being unreasonable by making the choice to relocate in my prime. I am sure they honestly felt I was passing up the only opportunity I had left for a wedding dress and a good life. Still, I felt an unrest from within me, so I kindly but firmly disagreed.

This letter was a call from the brokenness that **WAS** me to the wholeness I *COULD* be. After all the past shades that were thrown at me, mercifully, true love found me.

PEN THE POWER OF YOUR STORY

What are three things you know now that you wish you had known five years ago?

_____

_____

_____

_____

_____

_____

_____

_____

_____

_____

_____

_____

_____

Write about a funny experience of a relationship/date gone wrong.

_____

_____

_____

_____

_____

_____

_____

_____

_____

_____

_____

_____

_____

_____

_____

Write a letter to your 'Future Self'. In it, create a vision board of you.

_____

_____

_____

_____

_____

_____

_____

_____

_____

_____

_____

_____

_____

_____

_____

_____

Eden Adaobi Onwuka

CHAPTER #4
I Have Nothing More to Give

"When you get to your wits end, buckle up, rest, and begin again."

"I *have nothing more to give."* This is not a cliché or some fancy quote. It wasn't a one-liner from a blockbuster movie, either. It's not some catchphrase from a juicy tabloid. This was my life…in real time. Painful. Bleeding. Tired. Discouraged. Angst.

This was me speaking while hunched down in the white hallways of St. Joseph Hospital. Countless journeys to and from the familiar hospital had finally taken a toll on me, my expectations, and my strength. I could barely stand as I leaned heavily on my husband who doubled as a walking stick to steady me, while I tried to make it not-so-obvious to curious bystanders that I was in excruciating pain. We tried to get me into the car without rupturing my newly-stitched abdomen, but failed. I leaned on the car, all the while conscious of the fact that there was a police officer who kept glancing our way (perhaps he thought this was a case of physical abuse). In an attempt to get into the backseat of the car, I turned left, then right, then frontwards. It was proving to be an impossible task, as I was instantly reminded of the sore tissues, raw nerves, and my temporary 'handicap'.

I wasn't in an accident, if that's what you're thinking. I was a new mom. I had just given birth to my twin babies a week earlier. I had woken up from my drug-induced surgical haze and asked to see my babies. In response, I received polite smiles from the attending nurses who were intent on keeping me from being hypothermic or bleeding excessively. I pleaded with them to let me see my beauties or to bring them to me, fearing the worst had happened. They kept courteously stalling. Finally, I summoned all the strength my mum and I could muster to place me in a wheelchair and rolled my way over to the NICU (Neonatal Intensive Care Unit) where I saw my babies for the second time (I briefly laid eyes on them immediately after their births).

I was excited and anxious at the same time. I peeked into their glass beds and realized they were wearing oxygen masks. *"What had gone wrong?"* I wondered. The kind nurses assured me all was well but went on to explain they had been low on oxygen after delivery and required specialist care. As a new mum, my heart sank. After 10 months of carrying a pregnancy and with all the expectations, that kind of news immediately took its toll on me. I prayed and hoped for no other unpredictable outcomes. Multiple pregnancies are even harder because it takes twice the toll. I was looking at my babies and grew more concerned and confused when I saw a feeding tube in the nostrils of one of them. I later learned that she was not feeding and had dropped considerable weight — down to three pounds (1.5 kg) — which prompted the assisted feeding.

So, the journey started. Four days later, I was discharged with 'Twin A' in tow, the trappings of bringing a baby home, the requisite adjustments, and raging hormones of a new mum. Our phones were inundated by well-wishers who wanted to come see the twins, but both babies were not home yet — at least not the 'Twin B'. At the same time, I was still recovering from a medically-necessary surgery which left me totally dependent on pain medications and external support.

We had to care for 'Twin A' at home while making the daily trips to the hospital to feed, bond, and pray for 'Twin B'. During one of those trips, I experienced a level of discouragement I had never known after I read 'Twin B's' hospital chart. It showed a static result; meaning she had made no significant improvement. I noticed she still wouldn't eat, no matter how hard I tried. She refused to be bottle-fed and suckled weakly as I breastfed her. In that instant, I looked at hubby with pain in my eyes and said these words: *"I have nothing more to give."* I meant what I said. I was **DONE**: physically, emotionally, and mentally. I felt I had no reserve strength left.

I stood over 'Twin B' and spoke directly to her as she lay frail and pink. With tears in my eyes, I said, *"Baby girl, you know I love you. This is the voice of your mother telling you that it's time to come home. The incubator is not your bed. Your bassinet is at home waiting for you to fill it. Your nose was created by God for breathing and smelling; not for feeding. With all that is within me, I declare you are whole. Now, permit your wholeness to reflect on the outside so that the doctors can let you come home to us. I know inside your body is a Princess Warrior. I know your spirit can hear me. I want you to know how much we all love you. The picture is not complete without you. Please come home!"*

After that pronouncement, I explained to my husband I could no longer make the daily trips to the hospital. I felt I was breaking down and needed to stay alive in order to be a good mum to both twins. Thankfully, even though he tried to convince me otherwise, he didn't judge me. I pumped milk daily with the breast pump and sent it along with videoed prayers to 'Twin B' while hubby went every day to be with her. Sometimes, he went with mum. That break afforded me valuable time for my surgery stitches to heal, to care for myself, and to take care of 'Twin A'. A few days later, my miracle NICU baby started eating better. It was if she got a memo for a foodie contest! Soon after, she was discharged and came home to her waiting family...and bassinet.

That is why we must be careful not to prejudge others for snippets of their stories that we have no full knowledge of. Every childbirth story and experience are different. We have no idea the odds another woman has had to overcome in birthing her children. Childbirth in and of itself is tough enough without the divisiveness of the vaginal birth versus caesarian surgery debate that we engage in, let alone all the antiquated cultural misconceptions we allow to filter in. **I have always said that every safe delivery is a miracle.**

> *The validity of one woman's birth travail does not minimize the authenticity of another woman's birth travail.*

Every experience is poignant, and the outcome is more important than the process. In a sense, we are all 'Hebrew women' and must be allowed access to childbirth methods we are most comfortable with—without putting them and their babies at risk—and without being shamed into misogynistic perceptions.

Back to 'Twin B'. I was filled with joy as I carried her in our home for the first time. My heart overflowed with gratitude to God because almost a month had gone by since their birth. I was finally able to hold them in my arms together without wires, tubes, and fear. In that moment, I truly felt like a 'Twin Mum'. My heart was full. It still is. We grew stronger daily and the guests started pouring in. I also continued to heal daily. Each day became slightly better than the previous day.

> ### *Sometimes, the answers we seek can only be found in rest.*

Within five months after their birth, I began my studies and received a certification which had been a lifelong dream. I established a benevolence project for widows and was able to give more of myself, love more, serve more, help more, and stretched my limits even more — all by God's grace alone.

I went from being the tired, exhausted, bleeding, limping woman (who, at the time, had 'nothing more to give) to becoming the one seeking purpose-driven areas in which to serve. What changed? What made the difference? I honestly think that when we understand that seasons come and go and that we are also a priority — irrespective of the chaos and demands all around us—we can then avoid becoming casualties of "burnout".

Think about it like this: The big rig (tanker) that distributes gas to gas stations still needs its own gas in order to do its job.

In my tiredness, I had no point to prove to anyone. I listened to my body and my crumbling spirit. It was then I cried out for help. I sat down, hibernated, and suspended the rollercoaster flurry of activities. Doing so helped to revive, thrive, and restore my perspective. It also prepared me for the following months which were amazing and fruitful.

When my beautiful twins turned one, I found myself reflecting on the past seasons, the highs and lows, sleepless nights, tired limbs, stretched budgets, no date nights with hubby, multi-dimensional tasking, and loss of spontaneity. I became even more grateful that I had more to give.

We are limitless when we accept and embrace our limitations. We can get on the path to our breakthroughs when we refuse to break down. Sometimes, the answers we seek can only be found in rest. We need to pace ourselves, so we don't break ourselves. Tough as it was, guess what? I wouldn't change a thing!

PEN THE POWER OF YOUR STORY

How often do you rest? Do you have a scheduled time for rest?

_____

_____

_____

_____

_____

_____

_____

_____

_____

_____

_____

_____

_____

_____

Set a goal for a rest-and-relaxation pattern.

_____

_____

_____

_____

_____

_____

_____

_____

_____

_____

_____

_____

_____

_____

What role(s) will you play in eradicating childbirth misconceptions? Provide specific examples.

_____

_____

_____

_____

_____

_____

_____

_____

_____

_____

_____

_____

_____

_____

_____

CHAPTER #5
The Blessing in a Minus

"If you're not habitually thankful, you may never be consistently fulfilled."

I felt the cold, hard floor pressed against my warm face. I winced at the searing pain on my left hip and the numbness I felt in my left leg. I looked up to see my little girl rush out in response to my piercing scream. She was staring at me, partly amused and partly concerned. It was clear she wasn't sure if I had fallen or was playing an exciting game of peek-a-boo.

The reality was I had slipped on a wet patch on the kitchen floor as I rushed in to grab the next meal bottles for the twins. I had left them propped up on my bed with many pillows as a wedge. The makeshift barrier was necessary because they had become Sci-Fi Spiderman minions and wall-climbing babies, scaling their way over and through any hurdle. Their 'teamwork' left the house in a hot mess.

For a moment, my pain turned to fear as my life flashed before my eyes. I was home alone with the children and my phone was on a dresser in the bedroom, plugged into the charger, out of reach of any of them. If I had to call for an ambulance, I had no access to a phone where I had fallen. The doors had child-lock protection, so even my oldest child couldn't get out of the house to seek help. If I screamed, the neighbors couldn't hear me because we lived in a big house, and unfortunately, in Obodo Oyibo, no neighbor would 'accidentally' stop by to borrow salt or crayfish.

I said a silent prayer, mustered up every bit of teeth-gnashing, fist-clenching, face-tightening strength I had, raised myself up, and hobbled onto to my bed. Everything checked out okay. No major sprains, no split discs, no torn nerves. Nothing missing; nothing broken. Praise God!

Still...

I couldn't help wondering about the "What ifs?" *What if I couldn't get up? What if no timely help came? What if there was a broken spinal cord?*

> *Blessings are not in additions alone, but can also be in subtractions.*

Many times, we analyze our blessings in terms of additions: a new house, a job, a finished project, a new relationship, a contract, a promotion...typically, something that depicts a change in level or some visible measurable increase. We've been miseducated to believe miracles only come in relation to 'MORE'.

Please understand this: Blessings are not in additions alone, but also in subtractions. That toxic relationship that ended. The layoff from that redundant job. That dysfunctional relative who has taught you more about prayer than any prayer manual could. The nasty break-up that saved you from a broken life. That betrayal that taught you timely wisdom. Perhaps even the loss of something 'good' that could pave way for something great. Or the slips and near-fatal accidents like mine that you were mercifully spared from.

If nothing 'good' has been added to you yet, but something bad has been kept away from you, trust me: You are Blessed! If you have breath and still dare to dream, you are Blessed! If, despite your feelings of entitlements, you remember that some of the kindest, finest, youngest successful people didn't make it alive today, you should humbly declare yourself Blessed beyond measure!

Contemporary songwriter, Laura Story, in her song *Blessings*, echoes these sentiments:

"What if your blessings come through raindrops?

What if your healing comes through tears?

What if a thousand sleepless nights are what it takes

to know You're near?

What if trials of this life are Your mercies in disguise?"

Those Blessings you've failed to chronicle or be thankful for might have been a 'minus' you somehow missed. There are countless, unmerited Blessings in the 'minus'!

CHAPTER #6
When Your Guardian Angel is Also Your Twin

*"What are sisters for if not to point out the things
the rest of the world is too polite to mention?"*
~ Claire Cook ~

I was a team player before I was even born. I distantly recall swirling close to another mass of human flesh with our big, bulging eyes as we danced to the faint rhythms outside our first home: our mom's belly. We swam together, and oh, how we fought for food and rations within the placenta, which (by the way) we had to share because there was just **ONE**. We were roommates then but somehow, anytime food was ready, before I got around to eating, my sister beat me to it and ate it all.

Mom's amniotic fluid was our swimming pool; the oxygen she breathed the source that kept us alive together within her enclave for about 10 long months. I soon got tired of my sister taking my share of food, so I broke the lease on our shared 'rental' space and got out on the last day of April; a fragile baby weighing just shy of five pounds (2.25 kg). I guess the impact and guilt of what my sister had done soon caught up with her and, with the sudden realization that living alone in mom's belly was not much fun, she followed on my heels and soon arrived — exactly five minutes later that same day. I cried for joy and my twin echoed my sentiments as she sluggishly stretched out with her seven pound (3.25 kg) chunky self. We were born!

Our lives were pretty much gregarious because I have no throwback baby pictures of when I was alone. Funny thing: We always had to ask our parents to explain who was who in each picture. We craftily devised ways to temporarily solve the baby picture mix-ups. Whichever baby was fussy, unprepared for the photoshoot, crying, drooling, or had a weird expression had to be my twin. She retaliated by ensuring every childhood tale of the randy twin, the twin who slipped and scraped her knee, or the one who flunked the alphabets was me. After all, two can "play the game"!

Such was our lives. Our mutual struggles, pains, and setbacks made us stronger together. Although we haven't always agreed on many things, we complement each other in more ways than one — from sharing similar experiences through the same primary, secondary, and university schools to wearing the same clothes because my parents loved the idea of 'twinning'.

Our dear dad *(God bless his memory)* was a diehard romantic who, even when he couldn't find the same dress, would buy one in a bigger size and (poor me) just because I came out first, I had to pay the price. I was made to wear the bigger dress just because I was five minutes earlier than my twin. "Twinnie" would always look smart and feel smug in her nicely fitted dress (Show Off!), while I felt like a potato in a haysack.

We were like shadows and mirrors to each other because she gave me a perspective on myself that most people would pay handsomely to obtain (and vice-versa). Even when we were bullied in high school for years and friends turned against us while relentlessly trying to turn us against each other, we stuck together knowing we always had each other's back.

My twin's impact on my life has been as numerous as they come. She helps me get on course with my goals and saves my deadlines. After we graduated college and the list for our post-college internships came out, she got her National Youth Service Corps posting before me but refused to go until she shopped for everything she thought I needed and packed my suitcases, thereby saving me precious time. So, when my posting came out, albeit late, I could concentrate on leaving for camp without further delay. I was able to simply pick up the packed suitcases and leave immediately for Youth service!

Shortly after our service year, I had promising leads for jobs and even attended some interviews with Fortune 500 companies, but none had translated into an immediate job offer. When my twin got her first job, I was still unemployed and working pro-bono at a para-religious organization. She would graciously (of her own goodwill) share some of her salary with me. Every single month until I was able to gain employment (I was in an unpaid internship), she gave me a part of her salary so that I didn't feel unemployed.

> *"A sister is a gift to the heart,*
> *a friend to the spirit,*
> *a golden thread to the meaning of life."*
> *~ Isadora James ~*

It was not just what she did, but how she did it. There were days I would open my closet or suitcase and see an encouragement card tucked into it. Other times, there would be a good book placed inside and a check would fall out. She would consistently order lunch for me and give allowances to everyone else on my team on a regular basis. My twin didn't have much, but whatever she had, she willingly shared.

Twinnie climbed quickly in her career when I was just starting out. She also took her first international trip before me.

Still, it was important to her to share her joys with me. At the time, whenever she travelled abroad, I could count on getting a suitcase filled with goodies because she shopped exclusively for me. She ensured that whatever accelerated progress she had, I would partake of — including letting me drive her brand-new car at a time when I didn't have so much as a wheelbarrow to push around in my own name. Her generous nature taught me to share in the successes of others, even while I was waiting on my own success to unfold.

It didn't stop there, though!

Twin defended my honor among critics years ago, risking her own honor because the faith she had in me was bigger than the mess that was thrown at me. She is bold, stout, fearless, tells it like it is, and a tough businesswoman who doesn't mix philanthropy with business.

> *Angels have no philosophy but Love.*
>
> *~ Terri Guillemets ~*

She taught me to draw the line between compassion and common sense! Her organizational skills have helped me in my business and, because she is gifted with an analytical acumen and a great skillset with numbers, she makes sure my accounting books are in order.

My twin is my greatest cheerleader. Though a gifted writer herself, she celebrates my work as if there is no part two. She would file, save, post, and has tirelessly worked towards publishing me. She allowed my gift to blossom and flashed the spotlight on me rather than herself. She doubles as my editor and critic. She makes me rewrite my scripts and puts a brilliant spin on them until it becomes flawless. She does these things behind the scenes.

Her sacrificial support while obtaining my MBA in Boston, Massachusetts is something I wouldn't forget in a hurry. In the same year, she flew abroad twice — all expenses paid by her — to honor me when I graduated and as my Maid of Honor on my wedding day. Need I mention the planning and investment towards funding my graduate program? She is one big assurance from God that I will always have a faithful friend, a loyal companion, a second mother to my children, an avid supporter, a prayer partner who joins me on fasts (even with the shortest notice), my yab-mate, classmate, playmate, shopaholic mate, and someone who has undivided access to my home (just as I do to hers). I've left my babies with her to travel for important conferences without checking in on them because I knew with her, they would be safe.

The privileged access I had to support her during and after her childbirths brought so much fulfillment to me. The singular honor of allowing me to be her birth coach and witness firsthand the beautiful arrival of her sons is a powerful sight I will never forget. My children love her, and my husband is thankful for her. I love her children and remain grateful that our spouses understand that when we are together, they have to allow us to have our "us-time" while they go off to watch soccer somewhere.

> *Gratitude should not be reserved for post-humous ceremonies.*

My twin and I have an archive of vocabularies between us that would make even a linguist at a loss for translation. And because If I told you about the *'Agadus' who like 'kwok-kwok' and is doing 'omoligo' and is like 'fojfoj'*, you probably wouldn't know what the heck I'm talking about — unless she chooses to tell you. Words fail me to chronicle the depth of her essence. She has a strength, resilience, and goodness mingled with a twinge of sparkling mischief that could only come from her.

My twin sister is not just a friend, but someone whom I believe God placed in my life as a Guardian Angel. To know her is to know a loyal, faithful, fearless woman. To experience her is to experience a depth of unbridled goodness.

Why this story and tribute? I believe that death should **NOT** be the sole reason for tributes, eulogies, or appreciations. I recall years ago, as I sat brooding at the funeral of a good man and listened to all the good things people had to say about him over his cold, lifeless body, I silently wondered to myself how he would have felt if he knew that he mattered that much to all those people. In that instant, I made a decision to always let the people I love know they matter to me, when they matter to me, how they matter to me, and live every day with the consciousness that those who make a difference in my life deserve to be eulogized.

The Familiar can also be the Phenomenal!

I refuse to wait until we are well beyond 95 years old to let her or anyone else know how much they mean to me. Tributes are good at funerals, but they are great **RIGHT NOW,** too! Gratitude should not be reserved for post-humous ceremonies.

We all have a responsibility to recognize that God places certain people in our lives as blessings in perpetuity. They may be regular people. Ordinary people can carry within their wombs profound realities. They may well be unsung 'everyday' heroes or even family members we feel entitled to their love. Perhaps they may not have given much to you and their sacrifices may seem insignificant, but they are always there when YOU need them. Like a fixture, you can reach for them in those moments when "perfection seems" elusive. They may be regular people or appear ordinary. They may be familiar, but the Familiar can also be the Phenomenal!

PEN THE POWER OF YOUR STORY

How has your family structure or sibling relationship influenced you?

_____

_____

_____

_____

_____

_____

_____

_____

_____

_____

_____

_____

_____

_____

Describe a positive example.

_____

_____

_____

_____

_____

_____

_____

_____

_____

_____

_____

_____

_____

_____

_____

Share a negative example and the impact it had on you.

_____

_____

_____

_____

_____

_____

_____

_____

_____

_____

_____

_____

_____

_____

_____

CHAPTER #7
Still I Rise

"You may write me down in history with your bitter,
twisted lies. You may trod me in the very dirt,
but still, I rise."
~ Maya Angelou ~

Faint chanting in the background

"Awon eleye daa?

Awon eleye ree.

Eyin eleye daa?

Eyin eleye ree."

Stomping. Sounds of rustling feet closing in. Their chanting now at a feverish pitch. Their excitement was as tangible as their hatred. The thick slice of calumny could cut through heat of the arid climate in northern Nigeria. History has it that a few miles away from the village, 18th Century British explorer, Mungo Park, was buried. His grave lay peacefully in a simple tomb by the Kainji River. Kainji dam was one of the infrastructural masterpieces in former Kwara (now Niger state). It was re-allocated to the new state during the military rule and redistribution of states. I remembered the geography lessons my dad had given us as Yusuf, his driver drove his official car—a Peugeot 504—to bring us to New Bussa. He pointed to the changing vegetation and regaled us with brilliant lectures about shrubs, plants, everything, and what we were to expect with the bipolar weather in that region.

"Awon eleye ree

Eyin eleye daa?"

That chant cut through my brief reverie. I realized I had to walk faster in order to drown out the taunting noise closing in on me, except this time, I wished I could lay there in the calm Kainji River alongside Mungo Park. I figured any escape from the incessant torment that filled my ears was temptingly peaceful.

Fists clapping in gloating glee (jeers and muffled whispers)
"Awon eleye daa?
Eyin eleye ree.
Eyin leyee daaa? (tempo rising)
Eyin eleye ree."

Try as hard as I could, I could not block out the sound of this taunt, and though it was nothing new, it felt like the painful bulge of a familiar abscess which didn't go away, but made life unbearable. This had been happening for over a year spanning three school terms, but on this day, it had reached a dramatically dangerous climax.

What went wrong?

Circa 1991...

Passing the common entrance examinations after elementary school was a necessary rite of passage for anyone who wanted to be admitted into secondary school. Acing it with high scores gave pupils the opportunity to go to one of the prestigious Federal Government-owned boarding schools popularly called 'Unity Schools'. You chose your preferred school, though you never knew where you might finally be placed because admission was competitive and wrought with excessive lobbying. At the time, there was a great initiative to unify Nigeria and institute a love for federalism in students from a young age. It was a thing of pride to gain admission into one of these schools. The ritual of shopping for boxes, buckets, mosquito nets, bedsheets, provisions, math sets and textbooks, and cutlasses and hoes for agricultural time-outs (popularly called 'labor') was exciting!

The starched green and white uniforms, pinafore, and short-sleeve shirts with loosely-fitted plastic belts adorning the hips was not complete without a beret. Brown rubber basket sandals and chocolate brown leather shoes from the 'Bata' shoe company were recommended accessories. Fresh white shorts, multiple whole inner-vests, bra tops, nightgowns, sweaters and essential self-care kits were always part of the shopping list. It was not uncommon for parents to trim down the list to basic essentials if they felt the list was ostentatious. Cabin biscuits would invariably replace assorted cookies. Affordable Nasco corn flakes would replace the slightly higher-priced Frosties. Groundnuts would replace cashew nuts. Blue Band margarine would replace Anchor butter. But no matter what was taken out, Garri was one critical item that could not be removed.

Garri was a lifeline. The creativity of students ensured that garri—a local staple "foodstuff"—was a multipurpose culinary item that could be used as a meal, dessert, or snack. One way we liked to eat it was to soak the dried cassava grains in cold water, sprinkle it with peanuts, milk, or 'kuli kuli', and enjoy it. This exercise was known in slang parlance as 'smoking' garri. Some students discovered that if garri was deliberately left in water for a few extra minutes before consuming it, it would rise or 'swell', thereby doubling in size. Garri could also be made into 'eba' by mixing it with hot water, boiled with a boiling ring (which was considered a contraband item). Contrabands were items or appliances that were not approved by school authorities to be brought onto the premises, but students found a way to smuggle them in because they were 'necessary'. The eba could be eaten with 'geisha' (canned tuna in tomato sauce). Another interesting way we mixed garri was to make it into 'kwado', which is garri mixed with spices, sardines, and softened with a dash of water.

Once we arrived at school, we were assigned to a mentor or school mother who was responsible for teaching us the survival skills for dormitory life. They also served as protectors and mimi-mums and we (the school daughters), in turn, served them by running errands for them. Each school mum differed from the other, as they chose their style of mentoring which could be formal, official, laid back, or very friendly. My school mum was Abigail. My sister—who didn't have a pre-assigned school mum because she was a transplant from another federal school—had to be assigned to Christiana, the head girl. We dared not call them by name. There was an unwritten hierarchy which had to be dogmatically followed. Any student a class above was to have the prefix 'Sister' before their name, and those two classes or more above were 'Seniors'.

Most of the Seniors were intimidating in their style of communication. Sarcasm was a well-respected style amongst them. If they told you to walk away, they meant you shouldn't. If they invited you to join in their camaraderie, they meant you couldn't. We had the responsibility of learning their nuances, answering every question they asked, and not talking back when they talked. It was a cycle of life at the boarding house. We were newcomers who served our way to the top to have others serve us.

Different Seniors belonged to different cliques. We had the religious ones who groomed Junior girls to become their religious protegees. We also had the social ones; the ones we considered hip, fun, and secular. Then there were those who were prefect material, well-loved by the teachers and principal whom we fondly called 'Princy'.

However, the most feared of them all was a small percentage of mean Seniors who had identity issues and masked them by portraying a venomous, intimidating character and meting out high-handed punishments, threats, and vulgarities to Juniors. Everyone avoided them and, for some strange reason, even their mates couldn't call them out publicly. They could intervene and appeal for them to show mercy on any Junior girl who fell prey to their wrath, but the 'wicked' Seniors seemed untouchable.

When Seniors needed to send a Junior girl on an errand, we heard a loud call: **"I NEED JUNIOR GIRLS!"** That call was followed by a mini-race-and-shuffle and, oftentimes, the last or sometimes the first person to respond to the call had to walk the almost three miles it took to fetch buckets of water from the dormitory to the water pump. We were always on high alert.

These intense moments were punctuated by fun memories of buying tasty snacks from the truck shop. Clarita's popcorn, kokoro, matrons moi-moi, and Sunday bread were favorites. The bustle and energy we expended in stretching tiny hands into the one room spaced building firmly secured by wrought iron windows until you were attended to added to the excitement of it all. It was there that we learned lobbying and negotiating skills. One would gain an upper-hand if there was a friend…who had a friend…who had a friend selling in the truck shop on any given day.

The annual interhouse sports season was usually the highlight of the year. It included daily morning jogs in the biting cold, from the dormitories to the gates — a distance of almost 15 miles — chanting 'Man O War' songs, from exaggerated to solemn to animated:

"Who say we no go win?"

"Shalolo…"

"Nebuchadnezzar…hey, hey…was a king…kingey…"

Sometimes, the songs were as ludicrous as they were humorous, but the crescendo helped us jog every morning, house by house. Most of us didn't look forward to it, but we really had no choice. Once we heard the morning bell and whistle, we shot up and out of bed faster than a rocket.

There was a whole lot of singing. Singing helped us deal with the blues and the loneliness of being far away from home. From the time the school PTA-approved buses (Kwara Express) left Ojora, we tearfully stared at the receding images of parents and guardians as they prayed for us and waved their solemn good-byes to the 10-hour trip through several states, we sang our hearts out. We sang about everything, from love to heartbreaks to praises to traditional songs. We sang of our love for Lagos: *"Lagos ile mi oh ayaya, Lagos ile mi oh ayaya…"* It was beautiful, all parts sonorously represented. Singing was an important aspect of communication and bonding.

As soon as we settled in to a predictable school schedule, the mystical stories of roaming phantoms would begin. Tales of the school grounds being a former burial ground always topped the charts. The gist was largely unsubstantiated, but it made for good adrenaline-pumping stories—a stimulant we were badly in need of. Though I never saw them for myself, some students had salacious tales of a black phantom male named "Baba Dudu" who roamed the hostels, and a perky slain queen purportedly called "Madam Koi-Koi". Some dramatic classmates swore they had seen the ghosts, but we weren't sure they had not made up those tales for attention. There was also the category of students who regaled us with tales of bush babies whose cries pierced through the night as well as cowboys on horses. Haha! The tales were as numerous and endless as they came!

Such was the environment within our school; fun and fast-paced, serious and sensational, spiritual and superstitious. This became the breeding ground for all kinds of misconceptions, accusations, and counter-accusations.

The chants were now regular. It had started as occasional, but it now seemed like everywhere my sister or I went, there would be a mischievous group of classmates singing:

"Awon eleya daa?

Eyin eleye ree.

Where are the witches?

Here are the witches."

You read correctly: **WITCHES**. We were branded as witches! This falsehood inadvertently begun with some phony dream a classmate, Yetunde, had in the third term of JSS1. I still recall the malicious glint in her eye as she came to me and said,

"Adaobi, I had a funny dream about you. I hope you won't be annoyed if I tell you".

Being free-spirited and not giving much thought to it, gave her the time to tell me about her dream. She went on to tell a rather disjointed dream where I was supposedly laughing or running, then turned into a lion and began chasing her. Unfortunately, I naively laughed at it rather than scolding her and directing her to desist from teleporting me into a figment of her imagination. I laughed it off. It was a harmless thought, and I was young and naïve. I didn't give it much thought.

> *Bullying is a system of isolation using rumors, untruths, and distorted perceptions to victimize its targets.*

In retrospect, I should have because apparently, she shared this 'sinister dream' with other pre-pubescent hormonal teenagers. Each version varied from one person to the next, and by the time the story made its rounds, it became darker, twisted, and was not received as a dream, but as a "truth" that set in motion a chain of unpleasant events that made my life hell for almost three school terms. I would notice whispers, jeers, and hushed gossips as I walked into or out of the classroom. It all started rather subtly but grew more brazen with each passing day, adding more 'recruits' to their bullying gang. My twin sister and I were the unfortunate targets.

Among our peers, we were pretty outspoken and popular; however, bullying has no template or temperament. Quiet, loud, friendly, or socially-awkward people can become the target of bullies. Bullying is a system of isolation using rumors, untruths, and distorted perceptions to victimize its targets. It spreads from group to group and, by the end of the day, it is almost impossible to contain.

After dinner in the evenings, all students went to their classrooms for prep; a two-hour study period when we worked on assignments, read books, or prepared for next day's teachings. It was not uncommon for students to fall asleep during prep from pure exhaustion, and I was not exempt. When I got tired and fell asleep on my desk with my legs crossed underneath, I would hear hushed whispers and at least one brazen classmate would walk up to me and stretch out my crossed legs. They would clap and tell me to my face that I was preparing to fly on a broom. Apparently, they had gone to my sister's class and found her sleeping as well. Our similar mannerisms, which is a no-brainer because we are identical twins, were often misconstrued and exaggerated. I lost friends during that time because though some of them knew there were falsehoods spoken about me, they did not want to be on the other side of the popular divide.

Another remarkable incident which left me speechless was an honest girly banter amongst my school friends about how we missed home and our mums' homemade cooking. We all talked about missing Sunday lunches, which comprised of rice, stew, and chicken. Each person shared with gusto what parts of the chicken she liked best: wings, drumsticks, et al. I stated I liked the head (or the brain matter), and we all laughed.

> ## *It takes character to stand for the truth when the lie has gone viral.*

Imagine my surprise when the next day, a classmate called me out for saying I loved human brain matter! What? I looked at everyone who was there, expecting them to stand up for the truth. Not a single one of them did. They feared going against popular opinion, albeit popular falsehood. I was so lonely. All I had was my sister, so we immersed ourselves into our books, which paid off in our grades. We excelled academically, and our positions bumped up. When I took the second position in class, some of the 'groupies' were indignant. They said I did not work for it, but attained the position be feasting on 'brain matter'. Haha! They wouldn't let up!

They would check on us in our hostels while we were asleep. Soon enough, the story spread like wildfire beyond our classrooms. Some Seniors — ones we expected to know better — joined in to malign. As I walked into the hostel corridors, I would find them staring at me. I would respond with a smile, only to hear a mocking salute: *"Girl of the underworld"*. This continued and painfully cost us the love and goodwill of two Seniors who had become like mothers to us. Maureen and Juliet were caught in the middle, and I could not blame them for not knowing what the truth was. They would call my sister and me — each privately — coercing and expecting us to "confess" to participating in witchcraft so that they could exorcise us. This confused us even more.

Every day, I would meet up with my sister after breakfast, since we were in different hostels and classrooms. She would tearfully tell me how they warned her to be careful of me since they thought I was the witch and was trying to bewitch her. I was perplexed because I had also been called separately and strongly advised to be careful of her because **SHE** was the witch. When we realized that all we had was each other and that the rumors were aimed at tearing us apart, we became more determined to stay united and play along with the foolery.

In my prayer time, I became so sad and burdened that at the age of 12, I asked God to please make me a witch because I felt so powerless against the bullies. I figured if I became a witch, perhaps that would allow me to have some special powers of retribution against those who lied against me. Each term, we would go home and decide to tell our parents who were active in the PTA, but we felt so sorry for our classmates and did not want any of them to get in trouble or be expelled. We changed our minds each time at the point of talking to mum and dad about this.

Sadly, the secrecy fueled their negative energy. 'They' became *invincible*.

"*Awon eleya daa?*

Eyin eleye ree.

Where are the witches?

Here are the witches."

When I heard those chants again, something in me broke. I knew I could not take it anymore. Months of jesting, lies, misrepresentations, false labels, betrayal by friends, and gang-ups had taken their toll on my emotional health. This time, even if I tried, I would not survive any further onslaught from the bullies.

So, I began running. I ran as fast as my legs could carry me. I ran from the pathway leading to the laboratories until I reached the staff quarters. I stopped in front of the Home Economics teacher's house and feverishly banged on her door. If there was anyone who would help me "un-witch", it was her. Ms. Elosiuba had the reputation for being a disciplinarian, calm yet stern, and earned both the fear and respect of students and teachers alike. She was also an active coordinator for the school's Christian fellowship, so I knew that she might be able to help. It was a calculated risk, but one I was willing and ready to take. What if she brushed it aside? What if she did not believe me? What if she thought what they were saying about me was true? Whatever the outcome, I was willing to take a gamble. Anything apart from the systemic bullying and falsehood was welcome. So, a nervous 12-year-old knocked on her door. When she finally opened it, I broke down in her presence and narrated the entire ordeal. She was flummoxed and angry. She calmed me down and asked me to sit in her sparsely-furnished living room while she sent for the key players in the 'witch saga'.

When they arrived, she separated them and with each individual standing alone, she questioned the validity and wickedness of the claims. In that moment, the unexpected happened: All of them began stammering and pointing to one another! *"It wasn't me; I only repeated what 'A' said to me!"* *"No, it was 'B' who told 'C', and 'C' told me!"* "*I was not part of it. I...I...I...*" Their tough veneers crumbled. Behind the masks of bullying were insecure, vulnerable, misguided girls. The only strength they had was in theie collective ability to fuel the fire of falsehood, but when called out by a higher authority (in this case, a teacher), there was no center to cling to.

In less than an hour, the labels they had ferociously built and upheld came to an abrupt end. They were called out so much by the teacher, they all began to cry. I'm sure it did not feel good being on the receiving end of justice. I even felt sorry for them, yet the relief I felt soon overpowered that emotion. The teacher administered appropriate punishments on them and left everyone with a firm warning: If she was to hear any more about this from any quarters, they would all be expelled. That drove the point home. No one wanted to be expelled.

Everyone deals with incidents of school pranks, harmless banters, and mean classmates. It may appear that this was one of them, but it isn't. **Labels are dangerous. Labels get innocent people killed. Labels have been responsible for genocides, civil wars, and world wars. The problem with labels is that they sound lighthearted at first at the expense of the labeled.** In a society that is deeply spiritual and superstitious, a label like 'witch' could instigate others into a mob mindset. In a continent where occasionally, the minority ignore the civil systems and the rule of law by taking laws into their hands via jungle justice, labels have been an accelerant to violence.

Picture this: Imagine walking across one of the busy markets in Lagos when you suddenly hear an angry shout; *"Ole...Ole..."* There is usually little room for interrogation, investigation, or candid assessment of facts. In a series of fast-paced events, a lighter, some sticks, used tires, and fuel are presented. Then, unfortunate lives get cut short. Children become abandoned by parents, elderly parents are rejected by the very kids they raised, neighbors live in malice with other neighbors, and reputations are marred when there is a passionate, misguided inference to witchcraft.

> ## *Labels are for products; not people.*

We were all teens. We were all on the tedious paths of self-discovery and sucked in by impressionism. We were all young and hurt one another in dimensions we may never truly understand. Still, I had a choice. Like anyone who has felt the sting of betrayal, we do have a choice: to forgive or to hold them and ourselves bound by unforgiveness. I chose to forgive.

Even though I was very young, my parents had taught me The Lord's Prayer:

"Our Father in Heaven,

Hallowed be Your name.

Your kingdom come,

Your will be done,

On earth as it is in Heaven.

Give us this day our daily bread,

And forgive us our debts,

As we also have forgiven our debtors.

And lead us not into temptation,

But deliver us from evil."

(Matthew 6:10-13, KJV)

I reckon forgiveness did not mean they were exempt from justice; it simply meant I was willing to ventilate my spirit and allow healing to happen. It meant I was no longer willing to keep empowering those who had hurt me by letting them have a seat in my soul. They were no longer allowed to live rent-free in my head. It also meant that for me, what they did against me was not as important as what God did for me. I had been forgiven, so I could forgive.

The next few years were typical fun school years. Soon after, we finished high school. Most of us had moved far beyond that incident to become buddies; some, lifelong friends. A bright future was ahead of us!

PEN THE POWER OF YOUR STORY

Do you have an incredible school story? Have you been a witness to bullying? Describe both in details.

_____

_____

_____

_____

_____

_____

_____

_____

_____

_____

_____

_____

_____

_____

_____

_____

Recall a situation you found it difficult to forgive. What helped you move past the pain?

_____

_____

_____

_____

_____

_____

_____

_____

_____

_____

_____

_____

_____

_____

_____

Describe a situation that you believe the offender does not deserve forgiveness.

_____

_____

_____

_____

_____

_____

_____

_____

_____

_____

_____

_____

_____

_____

_____

_____

CHAPTER #8
The Bump that Prevents the Thump

"No discipline seems pleasant at the time. Later on, however, it produces a harvest..."
(Hebrew 12:11, NIV)

An animated toddler kept trying to reach out to me. She wanted to join me on the couch. She spread her smooth, chubby legs in a Simone Biles-like gymnastic attempt to climb onto the recliner—and exercise which had become her favorite pastime.

I gently tried to hold her, but she wriggled out in a cute attempt to reestablish her independence and climbed further up. In that split second, something happened...

She lost her balance!

With tiny arms flailing in scary confusion, she started falling backwards. It was inevitable that there would be a large, painful thump on the floor; perhaps even a big crash as the back of her tender head met the hard, uncompromising floor. It almost happened—but then it didn't...

Because of my impromptu mother's instinct, I lunged forward as she fell backwards to put affirm arm underneath her back to break the fall. My speed and the impact of her back against my hand made it feel like a hard smack on her back. She stared at me shocked, wondering why I had 'smacked' her. Then came the muffled cry. I comforted her and calmly explained to her that I didn't intend to 'smack' her, although it had felt like it.

At that moment, I smiled at the realization that we are often like my toddler, confusing a help with a smack; not appreciating a glitch when it should've been a disaster; and crying out in angst at those who try to save us from ourselves, all because we feel some 'pain'.

Tough love is still love.

We confuse the scenarios because of our limited perspective. We curse the 'pain', judge the 'pain', react to the 'pain', and misunderstand the 'pain'—all the while, not knowing that the 'pain' was our Savior; our Salvation. It was the pruning which preempted pandemonium; the fall which removed fatalities; the strife which didn't cost us our lives, and the 'smack' that separated us from the rest of the pack.

I couldn't help but wonder at all the times God— through mentors, detours, broken dreams, closed doors, and ended relationships—felt more like a whack in the back than some steady support; those times when the pressure of helping us not fall seemed worse than the fall itself. I smiled at the realization that many discomforts were just the bump that prevented the thump.

You see, tough love is still love. Learn to embrace the process. Stop resisting the stretch and elasticity that comes with expansion. Quit fighting destiny-molding bumps.

CHAPTER #9
Saved by a Song

"There is no co-pay for hope,
No hidden taxes. No surcharges.
Hold on to your hope. It is priceless.
The tiniest hope is better than dope."

As I laid on the stretcher in the dark hospital room, the faint beam of light from the computer screen and ultrasound machines the only illumination visible to me, I tried unsuccessfully to relax. The mild-mannered nurse circled me in an effort to make me comfortable. She propped my head with pillows, covered me with a warm blanket, and made small-talk as I got half-undressed. I reluctantly admitted to myself this time that I was afraid. A deep, gnawing dread left me tossing and turning the previous night, disabling my ability to get much sleep. I tried to pass it off as nerves, but that was far from the truth. I knew the difference between rattled nerves, butterflies, anxiety, and fear. This thing I felt was naked fear; a dark, brooding trepidation that almost made me question everything I had ever known about healing and miracles.

The doctor soon walked into the room with a warm smile, the edge of her lips curved like a smiley emoji. She was professional and had a kindness in her eyes that seemed to say to me, *"I know how you feel. I'll be gentle"*, so I exhaled a bit. She spoke calmly, explaining what the procedure would entail, while reassuring me that it would be quick and painless (though I would feel some pressure). She asked if I had any thoughts about the information I just received. I inquired about the implication of the results returning as positive. She explained that if the reports came back positive, it meant the cancer had metastasized. Metastatic Cancer. Two words which held an ominous threat. The fear of metastization was a nagging fear doctors and cancer patients prayed to never experience. It signified the unfortunate spread of the disease from the primary contained location to other areas or organs.

"How did I get here?" I silently wondered, recalling how just three months prior, I received a call with the diagnosis that changed everything. With no previous family history of cancer, barely nine months after I birthed my twin babies, I noticed a lump and went on to have my wellness checkup done. In a series of unfolding events like the flipping of pages in a tense moving plot, I made an appointment with a breast specialist, got biopsied, and received the stunning news: *"Ms. Onwuka, sorry to inform you that your results came back positive for cancer".*

My specific results showed Stage 2 Cancer, Grade 3 with concerns about the 'grade', which meant they considered it to be "aggressive".

Totally blindsided, I grappled with this new reality with feelings of confusion, surprise, and anger—a cocktail of emotions those who have received an unexpected diagnosis have dealt with—I also had feelings of shame. Yes. Shame. Not because being cancer-ed was shameful, but because I was trying to defend God's image in my head to anyone else who was to learn of my diagnosis later.

Like a devoted child, I was misguided in my thinking to believe that the diagnosis was going to look bad on God's "resume" (as though God was not mindful enough of me). After all, how could I accept that I was diagnosed with cancer so soon after my babies were born? One of my reactions was utter disbelief: *"But God, I'm not even 40 years old yet! Why me? Did I go wrong somewhere? Did we not pray enough? Could you not have prevented this?"*

Somehow, I managed to encourage myself soon after and went beyond those energy-depleting thoughts about a week later. I had to remind myself that my response or reaction would exacerbate or mitigate the impact the situation.

I had the following conversation with myself:

"Eden, if someone were to call you to ask for guidance on how to talk to their friend who received a cancer diagnosis, what would you say to them?'"

So, I took my own counsel, swallowed my own pills, and internalized the coaching I would've given a stranger, friend, or client.

I said to myself:

*"This is tough; I kid you not. **BUT** it can become worse with a negative mindset and bad attitude. Your perspective determines your narrative. What you magnify grows, and what you simplify goes — or at least it loses its power to control your joy."*

> *"Towdah" is the lifting up of hands in adoration, while thanking God in advance for things not yet received.*

Instead, I entered into thanksgiving—not **BECAUSE** of the cancer, but **IN SPITE** of it. I had a praise on my lips that had nothing to do with everything being perfect. I chose to count my existing blessings; those things I already had like access to good healthcare, a supportive spouse, and children while praising in advance for things I desired like good health, the right caregivers, strength, etc.

The Hebrew word for 'Praise' has several variants, each with a distinct meaning; but one interesting variant, **"Towdah"**, means to praise in anticipation for what we hope to receive. That was what I did. I believed that God could use my diagnosis to birth a new purpose, perhaps even weave a message of light to others who might need the encouragement I had received. That was three months prior.

Surprisingly, there I was yet again, grappling with the same feelings I struggled with in the beginning, all because the cancer suddenly stopped responding to the chemotherapy. I was on my 10th chemo-cycle of Taxol, when I felt heavier in the affected area. Choosing to not ignore it, I spoke with the oncologist about it, and he ordered a new set of ultrasounds. Sadly, they confirmed that somehow, despite chemotherapy, the lump had doubled in size at an alarming 100% increase. In addition, the lymph nodes surrounding the benign area were now abnormally enlarged. So, they recommended fresh biopsies midway in my treatment to be certain there was not a progression into metastatic cancer.

The helplessness I felt on that hospital bed had morphed into fear. Was this a death sentence? What was the extent of its spread?

Two days earlier, my friend Omo had graciously visited from Ohio and offered to drive me to MD Anderson Hospital. She tried to encourage me, but all the while, I had pretended the turn of events was not a big deal.

Now, lying down alone as I waited for the doctor, I knew it mattered more than I had admitted. It mattered because I didn't feel the usual reserve of strength I normally felt before every other procedure. I struggled to find peace which, for me, was the biggest sign of God's presence in my walk with Him. Peace seemed to elude me.

The past two months and the chemotherapy I had received every Friday suddenly seemed like a waste. All the side-effects, tiredness, nausea, headaches, insomnia, pain, and even the suffering seemed to have been senseless. It even seemed the prognosis was worse than it had been at the preliminary biopsy, except this time, I was a tired warrior who had already depleted most of her strength in the journey. The bursting faith I had stirred up before the treatments began was running out...fast. I felt like a truck driver who had run out of gas while driving through several states.

I looked up at the doctor and said to her, *"Please, could you give me a minute or two? I don't like how I am feeling, and because I am a person of faith, it matters to me not to proceed with this procedure until I deal with this fear"*. She asked if there was anything she could do to make it better. I had one simple request:

"Please, I need to play my favorite worship song."

I knew that if I permeated my atmosphere with worship, my spirit would be calm again. I knew that if I lifted up the name of Jesus, the storms raging within me would lose its threat. I knew that the aura of worship influences everything, and if I dared in that moment to wave a banner of thanksgiving, as ironical as it sounded, my focus would move from my situation to His promises.

Dr. Santiago nodded empathetically and said it was okay. I explained to her that I had tried to get the music to play on my YouTube for the past 30 minutes while waiting in the lobby, but my cell provider had poor coverage in the hospital. She responded with a kind offer: How about I tell her the song and artist, and she would search for it in Pandora on her phone since it used a different cell provider? I gave her the information she needed, she found the song, and put it on repeat. Tears of worship rolled down as the nurse gave me a towel to cover my eyes. In that darkness, I saw a picture of a grim future, death, and devastation. Then, the image turned around! With the rising crescendo of worship, I began to feel the fear fall away as the music, *What a Beautiful Name* by Hillsong United, saturated the atmosphere:

"You didn't want Heaven without us.

So, Jesus; You brought Heaven down.

My sin was great; Your love was greater.

What could separate us now? What a beautiful Name it is!

The Name of Jesus Christ, my King!

Death could not hold You.

The veil tore before You.

You silenced the boasts of sin and grave.

The Heavens are roaring; the praise of Your glory.

For You are raised to life again!"

The biopsy procedure began as I lost myself in worship. I immersed myself in the truth that death held no power before the Almighty. My faith came alive again, and I prayed fervently that God would make the reports stale; that the cancer would be metastatic. I declared His healing over my life and told myself repeatedly, *"He has not given me the spirit of fear; but of power, love, and a sound mind"* (2 Timothy 1:7, KJV).

The song played on and on. It was a song I had played from the first day of treatment and at every juncture; from port placement to biopsies to weekly chemotherapies. It held a deep meaning for me, and at odd times when I became anxious, the song popped up on KSBJ radio—the timing nothing short of Divine.

I managed a weak smile because there was shift going on in me. It seemed like it was not just the biopsy, but an exchange of auras. I felt the comfort and assurance of God's presence I had longed for. I felt peace fill me up. The biopsy ended, and the doctor and nurse briefly left the room.

In that instant, something happened. The song track somehow flipped to the next, though it had been put on repeat. Rather than change it, I chose to listen to the new, unfamiliar song. The following words filtered through:

"When You don't move the mountains, I'm needing You to move.
When You don't part the waters, I wish I could walk through.
When You don't give the answers, as I cry out to You;
I will trust, I will trust, I will trust in You."
(*Trust in You* by Lauren Diagle)

I felt a warmth I couldn't explain and started to laugh. The song was so apt. The words captured my exact needs and gratitude filled my heart. With my favorite song, God had restored my faith again. Through the lyrics of an unfamiliar song, God had moved me from faith to trust. It no longer mattered in that moment what the results would be because I knew in my heart that God only held in His heart what's best for me. I knew His purpose was more important than my reality. Although I wanted to be healed, I had also come to the point that 'even if' the healing didn't come in the way I hoped, His character was not on trial. He is a God of Love. With that, my spirit entered rest.

> *Faith focuses on the outcome.*
> *Trust focuses on who we become.*

Many times in life, we use conditions to gauge the love of a God who is limitless. We place conditions on Him with our broken humanity and our desperate conditions: *"God, if you heal my child…"*, *"God, if you give me a spouse…"*, *"God, if you break this addiction…"*, or *"God, if this goes away…then I will serve you"*, for instance. Here's the thing: **God desires to do a work within us that is greater than the work around us. He will put a structure in us that withstands the turmoil before us.** The tired, scared, helpless woman who entered that hospital room for her biopsy became the strengthened, peaceful, and trusting woman who rose from the hospital bed — and it had nothing to do with the results. In that moment, I still had no clue what the results would be since we had to wait a few days for them.

I stood up from that bed joyful; not necessarily 'happy' because happiness is transient, often based on happenstance, data, feelings, events, and people. I had genuine **JOY** that I felt was from above. It came from looking within at the faithfulness of God in times past and of His goodness from times before. Faith was good; yet without Trust, Faith could be depleted, and without Faith, there will be no Hope. My hope was revived with a song of praise. That song carried me through the next months of intensified chemotherapies, the loss of hair, darkened skin, heart palpitations, shattering spines, dizzy spells, blackened and broken nails, bleeding gums, neuropathy, and hot flashes. It continues to carry me through a segmented mastectomy, radiation, physical therapies, and hormonal therapies that may last the next few years.

> *And though we may feel helpless,*
> *we must never become hopeless.*

A few days later, the hospital called with good news: The cancer was *NOT* spreading. I was thankful for that. More importantly, I was thankful for Faith, Trust, and Hope. I learned later that the song by *Hillsong United was released a day before I got the diagnosis on January 7, 2017. I feel like it was written for me because it was going to be a crucial covenant anthem throughout my journey.

There may be times you'll feel like there's nothing worth celebrating in life right now. Look again within and stir your Joy! **Joy flows from a decision to trust a dependable God with the undependable circumstances you see.** Find your Joy. There's always a tiny trickle left, hidden somewhere in gratitude. Find your song. It might be in one that inspires life in nature, the innocence of a child, the foolishness of your mess, or your spouse; but your song will reconnect you to your strength. It will lead you—like David's harp—through stilled waters. It will calm you—like David's Psalms as he ran to safety from Saul. It will move you from a place of fear to Faith and steady you to Trust. Therein, you will find Hope again.

"And hope does not put us to shame, because God's love has been poured out into our hearts through the Holy Spirit, who has been given to us."
(Romans 5:5, NIV)

* *What a Beautiful Name* is a song by Australian group Hillsong Worship. It was released on January 6, 2017 as the lead single from the 25th live album, *Let There Be Light*. Led and written by Brooke Ligertwood and co-written with Ben Fielding.

CHAPTER #10
Ma...Eh!

"Look to the Lighthouse of the Lord. There is no fog so dense, no night so dark, no gale so strong, no mariner so lost but what its beacon light can rescue. It beckons through the storms of life. It calls, "This way to safety; this way to home"".
~ Thomas S. Monson ~

It was an island community, about two hours away when traveling by speedboat from Yenagoa. It reeked of locally brewed 'kai-kai' mixed with the lingering smell of fresh fish and the murky waters of the colored seas which surrounded it.

I had been given the furnished guesthouse, which was the living quarters of the aged mother to the Town Chief. Being the only female amongst a group of nine youth corpers deployed to Diebu Island, I was given preferential housing while the guys stayed in the Corpers Lodge. Five of us had initially been posted to a nearby community, but clashes between the community and oil rig workers made Peremabiri a risk-prone zone, so we were reassigned to Diebu.

This once-vibrant town with many modern infrastructure was now abandoned. Brazen pillars and buildings, now overgrown by trees and mold, had become a rustic playground for kids. There was a beauty to Diebu, however; the kind of beauty that came with an aged defiance because though the community was cut off from many basic amenities, the people loved to live loud. They were proud of their handiwork: fishing, hunting, and mild crop farming. They also loved to party, dance, and drink. Their famous dance was a 'waist dance' where they wriggled their hips rhythmically to drums or music. It was beautiful. Everyone—even the toddlers—seemed to have mastered the dance. Drinking was a favorite pastime, an accompaniment early in the morning while they played their board games.

There was a laid-back culture in Diebu, as no one seemed to be in a hurry to go anywhere. This trickled down to the women and kids. Everyone lived 'in the moment'. It was not uncommon to see many teenagers with babies and girls as young as 13, pregnant out of wedlock. People shacked up, had multiple intimate partners, and tried to make the best out of longwinding daily routines and the boredom that hovered over the island.

Prior to being deployed to the island, we learned the community school had been closed for a few years because there were no teachers. Parents pulled their kids out of the school, and the kids who had an interest in education were left as drop-outs. Grace Adua and her brother were two of the brightest kids I met while in Diebu. Shell Petroleum Development Company had posted me and two of the nine corpers to assist with revamping the school's system through one year of community service. It was a tough assignment, but one we were excited about and happy to undertake.

At the time, I was 22 years old, ambitious, and pleased about this opportunity. All the corpers each took two subjects; that way, all the subjects for the entire secondary school would be covered. I was to teach English and Literature for JSSI to SS3. I also doubled as a voluntary guidance counselor for the young students, many who had been sucked into the culture of unsafe sex, multiple pregnancies, and teenage abortions.

After school hours, I would host them at my corpers residence and listen as they shared their dreams, goals, and challenges. I began hosting book clubs, teaching them about self-worth, value, self-forgiveness, and affirming them. We spent a lot of quality time sharing, and the therapy sessions made some of them begin dreaming again. I was open to doing extra-curricular classes because I bore witness to a lot of promise in those who desired to read. We spent most evenings reading the Bible, dwelled on stories of redemption, and they learned how God is able to use anyone and that He could make something beautiful out of their lives.

In turn, they adopted me as their 'Big Sister'. They fondly called me '*Ma-eh*', since the Ijaw had a way of adding the suffix 'eh' to their words. They said I showed them that 'bukuru' was good: I represented the possibilities that an educated female could bring. They were generous to me, giving me some proceeds from their swimming and deep-diving. Fresh fish, water snails, lobsters, iguanas, and all kinds of exotic seafood were given to me from the fishing and hunting expeditions. They also brought vegetables and wild fruits from their farming.

Still…

Life was tough and lonely out there. We were cut off from civilization. There was **never** power and **no** clean water. I had exhausted all my drinking water and had to start drinking from the streams. An immediate consequence was that I became sick anytime I consumed that water. The streams were the only source of water, which meant that people bathed in them, swam in them, *and* hunted in them. It definitely wasn't the most hygienic water, so I found myself staying thirsty until it rained. When the rains came, we would put out every available container and bowl, managing to sift out fresh water that would last for weeks. Needless to say, we welcomed the rains.

I grew close to a number of kids, specifically three whom I mentored. In the course of mentoring them, they had committed to a living a life of purity and purpose. We all knew that would be hard because many of them had idol-worshippers and alcoholics as parents, which left them with no positive moral reference. I knew their hearts and desires for change. I was willing to help them as much as I could.

Whenever I traveled to Port Harcourt or Lagos, I returned with suitcases filled with books, clothes, relief materials, and sanitary wares. I loved those kids, and all the corpers ensured they had a busy school year. Parents began to send their kids back to school, and the community was alive again with hope bursting from the seams. The final-year students who previously did not have the opportunity to write their Senior School Certification Examination (SSCE) were prepared by us, and all of them passed their mock examinations.

We also volunteered in the only Christian church in the community; the Assemblies of God Church. It did not matter what denomination we belonged to, volunteering was a way we could teach the Bible to the kids and encourage them to learn. My fellow corp mate, Bayo, taught Sunday school lessons while I took the Ijaw praise and worship and part of the children's Bible study.

Ijaw is a *beautiful* language we found easy to learn, partly because on the island, it was a major part of communication. It had no consonant clusters, so enunciation was simple. My protegee students willingly taught me, and I was committed to learning. It was helpful in order to communicate with the parents and other community leaders.

One fascinating aspect of Ijaw was their names. I witnessed all kinds of exotic names. I met an elderly woman in Sunday school named 'Christmas' and a boy named 'Transformer'. I interacted with students named 'Education', 'Local Government', 'Borehole', 'Shell', and even 'Corper'. The students explained to me that names were sometimes given based on what was happening at the time of a child's birth (*I surmised that Madam Christmas was probably born on Christmas day*).

The tension between the villagers and the oil and gas companies whose rigs ran though some of the locales was acerbating, and though the community wanted us to stay beyond the National Youth Service period, it was not very safe.

We had been under either the Federal Government allowance payroll or were contractual staff with the energy companies. What *that* meant was that their liability ended with the completion of our service year.

I thought hard about taking some of the protegees back to Lagos, but after consulting an attorney friend, I was advised against it. The legal parameters were not in my favor because they were minors, and that scenario could later be misconstrued as kidnapping. I decided we would maximize the time we had and believed the seeds of light planted in them would bear positive fruits. It was emotional for all of us involved since we were just beginning to see the fruits of our labor bloom in them.

The service year was just about to end when rumors spread throughout the island that the Community Chiefs were planning to not allow corp members who taught strategic subjects like Mathematics and English to leave the island. They were unsure when next they would have teachers for their once-abandoned schools and decided to "hold onto" those already there. I was determined to finish my service to them and then return to my home in Lagos, but the pressures increased.

The Community Chiefs sent for me and requested that after my contract with the energy company, I remain in Diebu to work with the youths. I explained to them that would be an honor, but I had to return to my parents. *(Honestly, the volatile nature of the clashes and safety implications made it unwise to remain.)* The Chiefs seemed to understand, but unbeknownst to me, they had already decided to explore an "involuntary" option.

My protegees who had become loyal to me came to my room late one night and shared with me an incredible tale: They had overheard some Community Chiefs discussing amongst themselves that *"the only female corper* **[me]** *should not be allowed to board the speed boats, and that directives had been given to the boat operators"*.

> *What you rescue today might one day rescue you.*

When the information reached me, I thanked the students and changed my strategy. Most people knew I was leaving Diebu in two weeks and that I had most of my personal belongings and suitcases packed. However, I knew I had to leave **that night** if I had *any* hope at all of leaving. I called my student team and gave them most of my property and clothing.

I packed a knapsack filled with essentials and certificates, then disguised myself as a man. My protegees took me to the ferry at 4:00 a.m. the following morning so that I could catch the first speedboat out of there. That particular boat is usually filled with artisans, farmers, traders, and business people trying to make their early appointments in Yenagoa.

I boarded the boat and spoke to no one. The journey seemed much longer than it actually was. I held my breath, all the while hoping that there would not be any unplanned delays or a mechanical breakdown as the boat stopped by several nearby creeks to pick up more passengers. As we kept moving along—slowly but steadily—the darkness of the night soon gave way to the sunrise. The docks at Yenagoa came into view, but even then, I was still anxious and uptight.

When the ship docked, we exited one by one. The darkness was long gone, and we could see those on the boat clearly. As I stepped onto the slabs of the dock to finally stand on dry ground, an elderly woman who had sat beside me during the journey peered at me curiously while trying to make small-talk. She gave me a long stare and spoke these words:

"Ma-eh na you de dis? Hah, I no know say na our woman corper na im siddon for my side since. You come resemble man…"

I did **not** want to find out what was on the other side of her perplexed discovery. I ran as fast as my heavy brown corper boots would carry me. I made it back to the city. I was a bus ride away from the National Christian Corpers Fellowship family house. I was **two** bus rides from my home. I had served in Diebu with all my heart, and was now safe.

I am grateful for Grace, Mary, and her brother; and though they had told me how much they were indebted to me and how much of a blessing my mentoring had been to them, one thing they failed to realize was how much they had 'grown' me. They had taught me more than what I could have learned without them. I am truly grateful for their love and loyalty.

In a sense, what I had left in Diebu was **nothing** compared to what I had gained while there. The timely information from those precious youths prevented me from being stranded on an island against my will and may have saved me from a hostage-type situation. I could not help but be in awe of how God used them to 'rescue' me.

PEN THE POWER OF YOUR STORY

What volunteer experiences have you found remarkable?

_____

_____

_____

_____

_____

_____

_____

_____

_____

_____

_____

_____

_____

_____

_____

In what ways did you add value to your mentoring relationships?

_____

_____

_____

_____

_____

_____

_____

_____

_____

_____

_____

_____

_____

_____

Write a story that captures the theme, "What you rescue today might one day rescue you".

The Power of a Single Story

_____

_____

_____

_____

_____

_____

_____

_____

_____

_____

_____

_____

_____

_____

_____

CHAPTER #11
Chased by a Drifter

"The golden moments in the stream of life
rush past us and we see nothing but sand;
the angels come to visit us,
and we only know them when they are gone."
~ George Elliot ~

We all looked up to our father. He stood out like a dream. Always impeccably dressed, he loved the outdoors, too. When he was not at work or traveling on business tours, he was planting trees, jogging, or building something. We looked forward to spending Saturdays with him.

On this one particular day, he wore his rain boots and walked into nearby uncompleted buildings, surveilling the new estate we had just moved into. His double-barrel guns were slung across his arms. He came from a lineage of proud hunters and wrestlers, and polished his guns with excellent precision. We knew not to touch them.

He had always been interested in real estate. Being the visionary that he was, he bought lands in different parts of the country, believing that once-stale wastelands could become enviable cities…with time. That was what he had seen in Okota three decades ago. He believed that somehow, the forest-grown and weed-overgrown area we visited every week would be habitable. He convinced my mum, and they bought plots of land there.

As children, we didn't care much about big visions; we just loved the weekly rides from Satellite Town to Okota. The merry-hearted singing in the car led to a lavish picnic. It was so exciting! Dad would chant, *"Okota"*, and we would answer, *"Sosei"*, making us feel like comrades of his.

The area was thick with grass and weeds. It was not unusual for dad to alight and clear the path with his machete to allow us to drive through. He supervised the building and architectural designs, then laid out mats and recliner chairs in a cozy area where we spent time resting, playing board games, and having family time. In between meals, he would stroll over to the other incomplete structures to ensure there were no drifters there. The landowners were few but they were tightly knit, each looking out for the other.

The land in front of our property was waterlogged, and a wooden slab extended access it. Dad and I crossed the slab heading toward the buildings; him first and then me. As I stepped on to the right end of the slab, it had lifted up slightly on the left end. There was a *"splash"* near us that came from the flooded gutters. Wondering what the splash and ripple that followed was caused by, I quickly turned to catch up with dad.

That was when I saw an upset, almost angry-looking man who was wearing a brown caftan. There was a dagger visible on his waist — **and he was running right at me!** His arms were flailing around and his voice was raised in unintelligible screams. He was speaking the Hausa language and pointing directly at **ME!** I froze in terror and then let out a scream. That alerted my dad, who immediately rushed to my side while simultaneously trying to shield me and reach for his weapon. I was so sure that man was coming to harm me, and he was approaching *FAST!*

> *Life has no blueprint or*
> *stereotype for angels.*

A few feet shy of reaching us, he suddenly dived into the gutters and seemed to disappear for a few minutes. This confused my dad even more, and he pushed me to safety while keeping his weapon at the ready. After about a minute, the man — whom we would call a 'Mallam' because of their outfits or the fact they were nomads from Northern Nigeria —

resurfaced. Surprisingly, he was not alone. He was carrying the bloated body of my kid brother.

Shocked, dad put down his weapon, and both men proceeded to give him CPR *(in my young mind, it seemed like forever)*. Soon, my brother coughed and threw up a lot of water, following by crying. **He was alive!** He had been taken out of the gutter just in time.

What we did not know at the time was that my brother, whom I was very fond of, had followed me at a distance. I was totally oblivious to the fact that I had "company". The *"splash"* came from him stepping on the opposite end of the slab at the same time I had stepped away from it and then falling in. The harsh reality set in: I would have inadvertently drowned my kid brother and not have known.

> ### *Kindness is a universal language.*

The Mallam, a drifter who was a distance away, had seen my brother fall in and rushed down in time to save the day. *I believe his caftan masked the hero's cape he wore.* Dad invited him to join the family picnic and thanked him profusely.

That total stranger 'saw a need' we didn't even know we had, and although we didn't understand his language and were initially suspicious of his intentions, he sprang into action — proving yet again: Kindness is a universal language.

We may never truly know what an 'Angel' looks like on this side of Heaven, but one thing I **do** know is that there is no stereotype or prototype with angels. The 'Angel' we might meet or need may be *nothing* close to whatever preconceived notions we have of them.

I learned a lesson that day that stayed with me as I grew older: ***Not everything that plunges towards us is against us.*** On that day, the Mallam — that 'suspicious drifter' who chased us — changed us.

PEN THE POWER OF YOUR STORY

What stereotypes about others are you willing to confront?
Please specify two.

_____

_____

_____

_____

_____

_____

_____

_____

_____

_____

_____

_____

_____

Have you ever witnessed an unlikely hero? Describe the circumstances that made the person a hero.

_____

_____

_____

_____

_____

_____

_____

_____

_____

_____

_____

_____

_____

_____

_____

Write a story about how you did not allow misconceptions stop you from doing good.

Eden Adaobi Onwuka

CONCLUSION

Everywhere I go, I trigger a 'Faith' Revolution. I elevate perspectives and remind people their dreams are possible. I do this with compassion and creativity; with grit and garb.

Sometimes, it's what I say.

Sometimes, it's in how I say it.

Sometimes, it's what I write.

Sometimes, it's how I write it.

I walk boldly in my God-given calling because I believe involvement precedes evolvement, and destinies in despair can become realigned with their divinity. Even the undecided can finally find the clarity they seek.

This is my 'Why'.

This is my 'What'.

If one or more of these stories have stirred something in you, please get a notepad and pen and answer these important questions:

➤ What Revolution are you triggering?
➤ What end results are you instigating?
➤ Why do you do what you do?
➤ Who is your story empowering?

Look out for *Volume* 2! I would love to hear from you!

GLOSSARY

1. **Ada** – First daughter in a household; Ibo expression in Southeastern Nigeria.

2. **Agadus/Kwok-kwok/Omoligo/Foj-foj** – Coined "twin talk" and lingo which has encrypted meaning known only to the end-users.

3. **Agbero** – Derogatory term meaning thug or tout; word from Yoruba origin.

4. **Aso-ebi** – Uniform attire worn by a bridal party and friends of the newlyweds. Word of Yoruba origin.

5. **Baba** – Affectionate term for Father; word from Yoruba origin.

6. **Baba Dudu** – Translated to mean 'Black man'; a mythical male ghost purported to prowl through hostels.

7. **Baba Suwe** – Comedian and actor in Western Nigeria.

8. **Ejima** – Ibo name for twins; popular among Southeastern Nigeria.

9. **Eleye** – Flying birds; metaphoric for witches flying on a broom; Yoruba origin.

10. **Garri** – Staple food from Nigeria, West Africa; made from dried out fermented cassava.

11. **Ibeji** – Yoruba name for twins; popular among Southwestern Nigeria.

12. **JSS1** – Acronym for Junior Secondary School, equivalent to Form 1.

13. **Juju** – Mystical powers believed to exist in certain cultures.

14. **Kai kai** – Locally-brewed alcohol made from fermented herbs in Niger Delta.

15. **Kairos** – Greek for set time.

16. **Kokoro** – Tasty spiral snack made from fried seasoned corn grains.

17. **Kuli-Kuli** – Local snack indigenous to Northern Nigeria; made from solidified blended groundnuts and spices.

18. **Kwado** – A jambalaya-like mixture of moist Garri and spices created by students.

19. **Lobatan** – A definitive statement to draw home a point, like "That's it!"

20. **Moi-moi** – Steamed ground beans wrapped in foil or green banana leaves.

21. **Nine yards** – Metaphoric expression to express distance or length.

22. **Obodo Oyibo** – Living abroad or overseas.

23. **Ole Ole** - Thief

24. **Princy** – Slang pet name for Principal, commonly used in Federal schools.

25. **Skoi Skoi** – Onomatopoeic for the sound of high-heeled shoes on a hard surface.

26. **Smoke** – Slang term for eating or drinking Garri.

27. **Towdah** – Hebrew derivative for praise; connotatively of stretching out hands, lifting up hands in thanks for things that are and things hoped for.

28. **Voodoo** – Traditional magic or use of spells.

29. **Wound** – To "wound" a spoon; meaning to curve or bend the spoon into a 'C' shape like a hoe, which makes it easier to scoop larger portions.

30. **Yab-mate** – Jest partner.

ABOUT THE AUTHOR

Eden A. Onwuka is an International John C. Maxwell Certified Speaker and Trainer who delivers keynote speeches and coaching to aid personal and professional growth through study and practical application of John's proven Leadership methods. With extensive leadership experience and the privilege of being mentored by some of the finest leaders, she believes no task is too mundane and no goal too magnificent. She holds degrees in Bachelor of Arts and Humanities, and a Master's in Business Administration (MBA) respectively. She is currently enrolled for her Doctoral degree (PhD) in General Psychology with an Emphasis in Industrial and Organizational Psychology.

Her robust corporate industry experience spans 16 years in consulting and financial services with stints in Energy. She currently holds a mid-management position with a leading Fortune 500 company.

Eden is passionate about helping individuals gain the clarity and confidence they need to live life on purpose, and offers one-on-one coaching in the following areas:

➢ Relationship and Esteem: For mature single women, especially those who've been through a heartbreak.

➢ Creative Writing: For aspiring Writers and Thought Leaders who desire to hone their message or become published.

She is the Initiator of Adopt A Widow (A.A.W.), a grassroots benevolence project aimed at providing annual support to bereaved women beyond their grief period. In her spare time, she loves volunteering, traveling, and watching investigative movies. She writes under a variety of genres, from Leadership to Inspiration to Short Stories and Poetry (which she refers to as her 'First Love'). A social media denizen, she is widely-known for her thought-provoking nuggets and reflective one-liners under the brand name #SpeakerTrainerSage.

She is also the Author of *I am More than Body Parts*; a riveting memoir of courage and hope chronicling her journey from her cancer diagnosis to overcoming cancer, all written during her cancer treatment.

Eden lives in Texas with her husband and three beautiful children, whom she fondly calls her 'Shades of Grace'.

CONTACT EDEN A. ONWUKA

On the Web: www.edenonwuka.com

Via email: EdenWrites1@gmail.com

Facebook: www.facebook.com/edenonwuka

Instagram: @unwrittensage

Twitter: @dreden_O

ACKNOWLEDGEMENTS

It truly takes a village to groom a life. I would love to commend and sincerely thank the following people. This is by no means an exhaustive list, because I owe so much to others whom I may not be able to mention here:

- ✝ To the elegant, Godly woman whom I owe so much, my Beautiful Mother, Lady Oby Justina Ike-Udemgba. Witnessing your Faith firsthand and your strength in prayer have been great examples to me.

- ✝ My brothers and sisters and the Ike-Udemgba family who have always believed in me and celebrated my gifts since we were children.

- ✝ My Spiritual Mentors whose impartation and goodwill over the years grounded me: Pastor Ben and Ngozi Akabueze and Apostle Christian and Pastor Chinelo Philips. Thank you immensely, Pastors Gbenga and Inkky Olayiwole, Dr. Tony Rapu, Rev. John and Ngozi Okwok, Pastors Emmanuel and Crystal Asiwe, Pastor Moses Ida Micheals, and Rev. Mrs. Adenike Lamai.

✝ My Bosses and Mentors whose love and support helped make my relocation possible and, in turn, birthed some of these stories: Abubakar Suleiman, Yemi Odubiyi, Nigel Cookey-Gam, Akanimo Ekong, Esanye Mayor, Chinedu Igbokwe, Chinwe Eze Uzoho, Obinna Nwosu, Victor Etokwu, Ayodele Ogunmeru, and Moses Akinnawonu.

✝ My Coaches, John C. Maxwell and Dr. Aya Fubara Eneli, and these incredible women whose teachings remain a blessing to me: Bimbo Odukoya, Joyce Meyer, Beth Moore, Stormie Omartian, and Sheryl Sandberg.

✝ My Father's protegee, Sir ObaFemi Giwa-Amu, who bought my first laptop 10 years ago, urging me to publish.

✝ To Franca, in whose house the selfie that inspired this book was taken. Thank you Gloria Igbokwe, Gloria Omoregbee, and Joy Eneh for opening your homes to me.

✝ My Husband, Forever Gentleman, and Nurturer (FGN), Ambrose Onwuka. No words aptly capture the essence of who you are to me. Thank you, my Love, for making our home peaceful and conducive for us to pursue our dreams.

✝ My Amazing Princesses: Isioma-Mikayla, Anuli-Michelle, and Awele-Michole: That Heaven chose me to be your Mother remains the greatest honor I have received. Thank you for giving me "Mummy-Time" to write, when what you really wanted was for me to piggy-back-ride you.

✝ To in-laws, the entire Daniel Chinweike Onwuka family: I appreciate your love. You're the best anyone could have.

✝ To Angela Edwards of Pearly Gates Publishing, Houston, Texas; City on a Hill Center, Boston, Massachusetts; my church family at Lakewood Church; and the Marriage Rocks Class led by Richard and Sheri Bright: Thank you for your encouragement.

✝ I appreciate all the kindness, goodwill, and expertise that enabled me to birth this project. God bless you all!

Eden Adaobi Onwuka